Guide t

Practical Guide

V. Telman

Guide to Drupal

1.Introduction

Drupal is an open-source content management system (CMS) that offers a wide range of features and flexibility for creating, managing, and customizing dynamic and complex websites. With a large community of developers and a portfolio of modules and themes available, Drupal is one of the most popular and versatile platforms for creating business websites, e-commerce sites, social networks, forums, and much more.

Drupal was created in 2001 by Dries Buytaert as a personal project, but it quickly grew and attracted the interest of a wide community of developers and users worldwide. Today, Drupal is used by organizations of various sizes and industries, including businesses, educational institutions, government entities, non-profit organizations, and more.

One of Drupal's key features is its flexibility and scalability. With Drupal, you can create websites of various sizes and complexity, from a simple company presentation page to an e-commerce site with thousands of products. Additionally, Drupal offers a wide range of advanced features, such as multilingual content management, custom layout customization, creation of personalized workflows, and much more.

Another key feature of Drupal is its robust security. Thanks to its active developer community and ongoing security reviews, Drupal is known for being a secure and reliable platform for website creation. Drupal also provides tools for managing user permissions and protecting sensitive data, ensuring compliance with privacy regulations and data protection.

Drupal is also renowned for its flexibility in website design and appearance. With a wide selection of themes and modules available, you can customize the look and functionality of your website according to your needs and preferences. Additionally, Drupal supports the creation of responsive websites that automatically adapt to different devices and screen sizes, ensuring an optimal user experience on all devices.

Lastly, Drupal is known for its active community of developers and users. The Drupal community consists of thousands of developers, designers, users, and supporters who collaborate to continuously improve the platform, develop new modules and themes, provide support, and solve issues. Thanks to this vibrant and collaborative community, Drupal continues to evolve and stay up-to-date with the latest trends and technologies in web development.

Drupal is a powerful, flexible, and scalable CMS platform that offers a wide range of features and customization options for creating successful websites. With its strong security, design flexibility, and active developer community, Drupal is an excellent choice for organizations of various sizes and industries looking to create high-quality, high-performing websites.

2.Advantages of using Drupal

Drupal offers a wide range of features and flexibility for creating, managing, and customizing dynamic and complex websites. With a large community of developers and a portfolio of modules and themes available, Drupal is one of the most popular and versatile platforms for creating corporate websites, e-commerce sites, social networks, forums, and much more.

Drupal was created in 2001 by Dries Buytaert as a personal project, but it quickly grew and attracted the interest of a wide community of developers and users worldwide. Today, Drupal is used by organizations of various sizes and sectors, including businesses, educational institutions, government agencies, non-profit organizations, and more.

One of the key features of Drupal is its flexibility and scalability. With Drupal, you can create websites of various sizes and complexity, from a simple corporate presentation page to an e-commerce site with thousands of products. Additionally, Drupal offers a wide range of advanced features, such as multilingual content management, customization of layouts, creation of custom workflows, and much more.

Another key feature of Drupal is its robust security. Thanks to its active developer community and ongoing security reviews, Drupal is known to be a secure and reliable platform for creating websites. Drupal also provides tools for managing user permissions and protecting sensitive data, ensuring compliance with privacy regulations and data protection laws.

Drupal is also known for its flexibility in website design and appearance. With a wide selection of themes and modules available, you can customize the look and functionality of the website according to your needs and preferences. Additionally, Drupal supports the creation of responsive websites, which automatically adapt to different devices and screen sizes, ensuring an optimal user experience on all devices.

Finally, Drupal is known for its active community of developers and users. The Drupal community consists of thousands of developers, designers, users, and supporters who collaborate to continuously improve the platform, develop new modules and themes, provide support, and solve problems. Thanks to this vibrant and collaborative community, Drupal continues to evolve and stay abreast of the latest trends and technologies in web development.

Drupal is a powerful, flexible, and scalable CMS platform that offers a wide range of features and customization possibilities for creating successful websites. With its robust security, design flexibility, and active developer community, Drupal is an excellent choice for organizations of various sizes and sectors looking to create high-quality and high-performing websites.

3.Installing Drupal

Drupal is an open source content management system (CMS) that offers a wide range of features and flexibility for creating, managing, and customizing dynamic and complex websites. With a large community of developers and a portfolio of modules and themes available, Drupal is one of the most popular and versatile platforms for creating corporate websites, e-commerce sites, social networks, forums, and much more.

Drupal was created in 2001 by Dries Buytaert as a personal project, but it quickly grew and attracted the interest of a wide community of developers and users worldwide. Today, Drupal is used by organizations of various sizes and sectors, including businesses, educational institutions, government entities, non-profit organizations, and more.

One of Drupal's main features is its flexibility and scalability. With Drupal, it is possible to create websites of various sizes and complexity, from a simple corporate presentation page to an e-commerce site with thousands of products. Additionally, Drupal offers a wide range of advanced features, such as multilingual content management, customized layouts, creation of custom workflows, and much more.

Another key feature of Drupal is its robust security. Thanks to its active community of developers and ongoing security reviews, Drupal is known for being a secure and reliable platform for creating websites. Drupal also provides tools for managing user permissions and protecting sensitive data, ensuring compliance with privacy regulations and data protection.

Drupal is also known for its flexibility in website design and appearance. With a wide selection of themes and modules available, it is possible to customize the look and functionality of the website according to one's needs and preferences. Additionally, Drupal supports the creation of responsive websites, which automatically adapt to different devices and screen sizes, ensuring an optimal user experience on all devices.

Finally, Drupal is known for its active community of developers and users. The Drupal community is made up of thousands of developers, designers, users, and supporters who collaborate to continuously improve the platform, develop new modules and themes, provide support, and solve issues. Thanks to this vibrant and collaborative community, Drupal continues to evolve and stay up-to-date with the latest trends and technologies in web development.

Drupal is a powerful, flexible, and scalable CMS platform that offers a wide range of features and customization possibilities for creating successful websites. With its robust security, design flexibility, and active community of developers, Drupal is an excellent choice for organizations of various sizes and sectors looking to create high-quality and high-performing websites.

4.Creating a Drupal database

Drupal supports the creation and management of a wide range of content, including web pages, articles, blogs, forums, e-commerce, and much more. One of Drupal's most powerful features is its flexibility and customization, thanks to its modular architecture that allows developers to extend and customize the software to fit the specific needs of a project.

To create a database in Drupal, it is necessary to follow some fundamental steps that allow for the efficient organization and management of the website's data. In this article, we will provide a detailed overview of how to create a database in Drupal, from initial settings to content structuring and data management.

1. Installing Drupal: The first step in creating a database in Drupal is to install the software on the web server. You can download the latest version of Drupal from the official

website and follow the installation instructions to configure the website. During the installation process, you will be prompted to configure the MySQL or MariaDB database that will be used to store the website's data.

2. Database configuration: After installing Drupal on the web server, it is necessary to configure the database to start creating content on the website. To do this, you can use the database management tool included in the server control panel or use a graphical interface to access and manage the database. It is important to create a separate database for the website to ensure data security and organization.

3. Creating tables and fields: Once the database is configured, you can create the tables and fields necessary to store the website's data. Drupal uses a system of fields and tables to organize website content and information in a structured way. You can use Drupal's field management feature to define the custom fields needed for different types of

content on the website, such as titles, text, images, links, and more.

4. Creating content types: After defining the fields and tables in the database, you can create content types to organize the website's content into logical categories and sections. Content types are predefined templates that make it easy to create new content on the website and define the information and fields that should be included in each type of content. For example, you can create content types for articles, pages, events, products, and more.

5. Creating views: One of Drupal's most powerful features is the ability to create custom views to display and filter website content based on specific criteria. Views allow you to extract and display data from the database flexibly and customarily, allowing users to easily explore and navigate between website content. You can create views to show the latest articles, best-selling products, upcoming events, and more.

6. Data management: Once the database is created and the necessary content types, fields, and views are defined for the website, you can start managing the data and creating new content. Drupal provides an intuitive user interface for creating, editing, and publishing content on the website, allowing users to insert text, images, videos, links, and more. You can use revision and access control features to effectively manage website content.

7. Backup and data migration: It is important to regularly create backups of the database to ensure the security of the website's data and prevent the loss of important information. You can use the automatic backup tools included in the web server or use a third-party backup utility.

5.Creation of a new Drupal website

Creating a new Drupal website is a process that involves several stages and skills. Initially, it is important to have a clear understanding of the site's objectives and requirements, defining its target audience, necessary content, and required functionalities. Once these elements are established, the actual site creation can proceed.

The first stage of creating a new Drupal website involves planning and design. In this stage, it is crucial to define the site's structure by creating a wireframe that represents the layout of content, menus, and functionalities. The graphic style of the site must also be defined, choosing colors, fonts, and styles that reflect the brand's identity. Additionally, it is important to establish the hierarchy and organization of content by creating a site map that guides users' navigation paths.

Once the design stage is completed, the development stage of the Drupal website can begin. In this phase, the templates and modules necessary to implement the previously defined design are created. The templates will define the structure and layout of content on the page, while the modules will add specific functionalities such as contact forms, slideshows, or blogs. It is important that all modules and templates are developed to be compatible with the chosen version of Drupal for the website.

During the development of the Drupal website, it is essential to consider best SEO practices to ensure good visibility on search engines. This includes optimizing content, using friendly URLs, and creating a robots.txt file to indicate which pages should be indexed by search engines. It is also crucial to implement security measures, such as using SSL certificates to protect users' sensitive data.

Once the development stage is completed, the testing and debugging phase of the Drupal website can begin. It is important to test the site on various devices and browsers to ensure responsiveness and correct display on all devices. During testing, any bugs or usability issues that could compromise the user experience must be identified and promptly resolved. It is advisable to involve beta users to receive feedback and suggestions on how to improve the site before launch.

Once testing is complete and any issues are resolved, the Drupal website can be launched. During the launch, it is important to make a full backup of the site to prevent data loss during transfer. Additionally, it is recommended to inform search engines of the new site by creating an XML map and submitting a sitemap. After the launch, it is important to monitor the site's performance using analytics tools like Google Analytics to evaluate traffic, engagement, and user conversions.

After launching the Drupal website, it is crucial to keep it updated and optimized to ensure high performance and a good user experience. This includes regularly applying security and functionality updates, creating new and quality content, and constantly monitoring the site's performance. Additionally, it is important to consider user feedback and make any necessary changes to improve the user experience and achieve the set goals.

Creating a new Drupal website requires careful planning, advanced technical skills, and a methodical approach. It is essential to clearly define the site's objectives and requirements, design effective structure and design, develop and test the site accurately, and constantly keep it updated and optimized. By following these steps and best practices, a successful Drupal website can be created that generates traffic, engages users, and achieves set goals.

This is just a brief summary of the stages and activities involved in creating a new Drupal website. Every project is unique and requires thorough planning and customization to achieve desired results. Creating a Drupal website is an exciting and rewarding challenge that can lead to increased online visibility, conversions, and user satisfaction.

6. Drupal Dashboard

Drupal is an open-source Content Management System (CMS) that offers a wide range of features for creating and managing websites. Its administration system, known as the Drupal Dashboard, is designed to simplify the site management process and provide users with a comprehensive overview of ongoing activities.

The Drupal Dashboard is the main administration page of the site, which can be accessed once logged in as an administrator. From here, users can manage all aspects of the site, such as creating content, configuring site settings, managing users, and much more.

The Drupal dashboard is composed of several key elements, each providing essential information and tools to facilitate site management. At the center of the page is a summary of recent activities, showing the latest content created, modified, or deleted, as well as actions by registered users.

At the top of the page are the main menus, which allow access to various sections of the site, such as the "Content" menu for managing site content, the "Users" menu for managing user accounts, and the "Configuration" menu for customizing site settings.

On the side of the dashboard are information blocks, providing additional data on different areas of the site. For example, the "Site Statistics" block displays the number of registered users, site visits, and other relevant information, while the "Notifications" block provides alerts about any issues or important updates.

One of the most useful aspects of the Drupal dashboard is the ability to customize the layout and content according to individual needs. Administrators can add new information blocks, move existing blocks, and configure displays to create a tailored dashboard.

Additionally, the Drupal dashboard also offers analysis and monitoring tools to track site performance. Administrators can view detailed reports on site traffic, most visited pages, traffic sources, and more, to make informed decisions about site management.

The Drupal Dashboard is a powerful and flexible tool that provides administrators with all the resources needed to successfully manage a website. With its advanced features, intuitive interface, and customization capabilities, the Drupal Dashboard is an essential tool for efficiently and professionally managing a website.

7.Content Management

Drupal is an open-source Content Management System (CMS) that provides a flexible and scalable platform for creating and managing websites of any size and complexity. With over one million active websites and a large community of developers and designers, Drupal is one of the most widely used CMS in the world.

Content management in Drupal is an intuitive and flexible process that allows users to easily create, edit, and organize the content of their website. Thanks to its modular structure, Drupal offers a wide range of features and tools for content management, enabling users to customize their website according to their needs and preferences.

One of the key features of Drupal is the concept of "nodes", which represent individual content units such as pages, articles, blog posts, products, and more. Each node can be customized with specific fields and attributes, allowing users to organize and present their content clearly and structured.

Creating new content in Drupal is a simple and intuitive process, allowing users to add text, images, videos, and other types of content easily. With the integrated text editor and available add-on modules, users can format and style their content professionally and attractively.

Content management in Drupal also includes advanced features such as content revision, which allows users to review and approve content changes before they are published on the website. Additionally, Drupal offers a permissions and roles system that allows administrators to define who can create, edit, and publish content on the website, ensuring complete control over content management.

To organize and categorize content, Drupal offers a powerful taxonomy feature that allows users to create custom vocabularies and assign tags and categories to their content. This way, users can organize their content logically and intuitively, making navigation and searching easier for website users.

Thanks to its modular structure and wide range of available modules, Drupal offers unparalleled flexibility in content management. Users can customize and extend Drupal's functionality by adding additional modules for social media integrations, e-commerce, SEO, multilingual support, and more. This way, users can create a customized website that meets their business needs and goals.

Content management in Drupal also includes advanced features for managing images and files, allowing users to easily upload, organize, and manage all types of media on their website. With features like thumbnail management, automatic image resizing, and integration with external hosting services, Drupal offers an intuitive and efficient media management experience.

Additionally, Drupal offers advanced version control and workflow management features, allowing users to track content changes, collaborate with other users, and efficiently manage review and approval processes. These features are particularly useful for websites with complex workflows and distributed teams.

Content management in Drupal also includes integrated analytics and monitoring tools, allowing users to track the performance of their content, monitor website traffic, and gain valuable insights to improve user experience and increase engagement. With features like built-in reporting, viewing statistics, and integrations with external analytics tools, Drupal provides users with all the information they need to make informed decisions about content management.

With a wide range of features and advanced tools, Drupal offers users everything they need to create and manage successful, high-quality websites.

8. Creating pages and articles and Managing taxonomies in Drupal

Drupal is an open-source Content Management System (CMS) that offers a wide range of features for creating, managing, and publishing content online. With Drupal, you can create highly customized pages and articles and organize them using taxonomies.

In this article, we will explore in detail how to create pages and articles in Drupal and how to manage taxonomies to effectively organize content.

Creating pages and articles in Drupal

To create a new page in Drupal, simply access the "Structure" section of the admin panel and select "Pages." From here, you can create a new page by clicking on "Add page" and filling in the required fields such as the title and text of the page. You can also add images, videos, and other media to the page to make it more visually appealing and interactive.

To create a new article in Drupal, you can access the "Content" section of the admin panel and select "Articles." From here, you can create a new article by clicking on "Add article" and filling in the required fields such as the title, article text, and publication date. Like with pages, you can add media to the article to enhance it and make it more engaging for users.

Managing taxonomies in Drupal

Taxonomies in Drupal are a content classification system that allows you to organize content into categories and subcategories to make them easier to find and navigate. Taxonomies can be used to categorize pages, articles, and other types of content based on themes, topics, or other classification criteria.

To manage taxonomies in Drupal, you can access the "Structure" section of the admin panel and select "Taxonomy." From here, you can create new taxonomies and add terms to existing taxonomies. Terms can be organized in a tree structure to create categories and subcategories of content.

Once taxonomies and terms are created, they can be assigned to content during the creation or editing of pages, articles, or other types of content. This allows you to organize and classify content in a consistent and structured way, making navigation and search easier for users.

Creating pages and articles and managing taxonomies are fundamental features of Drupal that allow you to organize and publish content effectively. Creating customized and well-structured pages and articles can help capture the attention of users and convey clear and persuasive messages. Managing taxonomies allows you to organize content into categories and subcategories to make navigation and search more intuitive and effective.

Using Drupal for content creation and management can ensure a high-quality user experience and maximize user engagement on the website. Drupal offers a wide range of tools and features for creating, organizing, and publishing content effectively, making it an ideal choice for anyone looking to create a professional and well-structured website.

9.Customization of theme selection and installation of a Drupal theme

Customizing a theme on Drupal is an essential process to create a unique and personalized website. Choosing the right theme is crucial to ensure good design and optimal user experience. In this process, it is important to evaluate various aspects such as compatibility with the version of Drupal in use, ease of customization, presence of additional features, and the quality of support offered by the theme provider.

Before starting the customization of the theme, it is necessary to choose the theme that best suits the project's needs. Drupal offers a wide range of free and paid themes that cover different sectors and design styles. You can consult the Drupal Theme Repository to search for the theme that best fits your needs. Once the theme has been identified, you can proceed with the installation.

Installing a theme on Drupal is a simple process and can be done directly from the platform. After downloading the theme file to your computer, you can upload it to Drupal through the "Appearance" section in the administration menu. After uploading the file, you can activate the theme to make it visible on the website.

Once the theme is installed, you can begin customization to adapt it to the specific needs of the project. Customizing a theme on Drupal can include various aspects such as modifying the layout, choosing colors, customizing menus, managing widgets, and much more. There are various tools and modules that can be used to simplify the customization process and improve the site's design.

One of the most commonly used tools for customizing a theme on Drupal is Theme Settings, which allows you to modify the basic settings of the theme such as colors, fonts, layout style, and more. Through Theme Settings, you can customize the theme quickly and easily, without the need to know code.

For more advanced customizations, you can use CSS to make changes directly to the theme code. Drupal offers the ability to create a custom CSS file that overrides the default style rules of the theme. This allows you to create a unique and personalized design for the website.

In addition to CSS, you can also use customization modules to add additional functionality to the theme. There are modules that allow you to integrate photo galleries, sliders, contact forms, and more directly into the theme. These modules allow you to improve the appearance and functionality of the website easily and without the need to write code.

Customizing a theme on Drupal is an ongoing process that requires time and patience. It is important to test every change made to ensure that the website is functional and meets the needs of users. Additionally, it is advisable to always keep the theme and modules used up to date to ensure security and compatibility with the latest versions of Drupal.

Customizing a theme on Drupal is a fundamental process to create a unique and personalized website. Choosing the right theme, installing it correctly, and customizing it appropriately are essential steps to ensure an attractive design and a good user experience. With the right tools and modules, you can create a unique and functional design that meets the specific needs of the project.

10. Extending Drupal with Modules

Drupal is one of the most widely used CMS in the world, thanks to its flexibility and customization. One of the main strengths of this tool is its extension through the installation of modules. Modules are small software components that add extra functionality to the core of Drupal. They can be developed by the community or third parties and can be downloaded and installed with a few clicks directly from the Drupal administration panel.

Extending Drupal with modules allows you to completely customize the website, adding specific functionalities according to the user's needs. Modules can be used to add functionalities such as forums, e-commerce, blogs, photo galleries, product listings, newsletters, contact forms, events, interactive maps, and much more.

There are thousands of modules available for

Drupal, each offering specific functionalities and can be customized to fit the needs of the website. The wide range of modules available allows developers to create highly personalized and functional websites without the need to write code from scratch.

One of the most popular modules for Drupal is Views, which allows users to easily create custom views of the content on the site. With Views, you can select which fields to display, how to arrange them, and which filters to apply to filter content based on certain criteria.

Another widely used module is Pathauto, which automatically generates search engine-friendly URLs for new content created on the site. Pathauto allows you to define rules for URL creation, simplifying the SEO optimization process of the site.

Other popular modules include Webform, which allows you to create custom contact forms, Token, which allows you to insert dynamic variables into different elements of the site, and CKEditor, which replaces Drupal's default text editor with a customizable WYSIWYG editor.

Drupal modules can be divided into different categories based on their functionality. For example, there are modules for site administration, such as Drush, which allows you to manage the site directly from the command line, security modules like Security Kit that protect the site from cyber attacks, and social media integration modules like Social Media Links that allow you to add sharing buttons to site content.

Furthermore, Drupal modules can be combined to create complex and highly customized functionalities. For example, you can use the Views module in combination with the Date module to create a view that displays future events, allowing users to filter them by date and event type.

The wide availability of modules for Drupal allows developers to create highly customized and functional websites quickly and efficiently. The Drupal community is very active and offers constant support and updates for available modules, ensuring that the CMS remains up to date and able to meet the needs of users.

Extending Drupal with modules is a fundamental aspect of creating personalized and functional websites. The wide range of modules available allows users to add extra functionalities to their site easily and quickly, without the need to write code from scratch. Thanks to modules, Drupal remains one of the most powerful and flexible CMS on the market, capable of meeting the needs of any type of web project.

11.Creating new users in Drupal

Drupal is an open source content management system that offers many advanced features for creating and managing dynamic websites. One of the most important features of Drupal is the ability to easily create and manage new users, allowing them to access the site and interact with specific content and features.

To create a new user in Drupal, you first need to access the site's administration area and go to the section dedicated to user management. Once there, you can view all the users already registered and create new users by clicking on the "Add user" button.

Within the new user creation form, you can enter all the necessary information to identify and distinguish the new user, such as name, last name, email address, role, and specific permissions. Additionally, you can set a temporary password for the new user, which will need to be changed upon first login.

45

One of the most interesting aspects of creating new users in Drupal is the ability to define roles and specific permissions for each user. Roles allow you to define groups of users with different privileges and permissions, effectively managing the security and privacy of the website.

Permissions, on the other hand, allow you to define specific actions that a user can perform on the site, such as editing content, publishing articles, or accessing certain reserved sections. Thanks to this flexibility, you can create users with different levels of access and privileges, ensuring precise control over the activities carried out on the site.

Once the new user has been created, you can send them a confirmation email containing instructions on how to access the site and set their password. After completing this procedure, the new user will be able to access the site and use the available features and content, based on the roles and permissions defined during creation.

Furthermore, Drupal offers the possibility to customize the experience of registered users through the use of additional modules, such as modules for managing user profiles, creating custom reserved areas, or implementing feedback and social interaction systems.

Creating new users in Drupal is therefore a fundamental process to ensure a rich and personalized user experience, allowing for effective management of user access and interaction with the website. Thanks to the flexibility and advanced features offered by Drupal, it is easy to create and manage a dynamic and engaging online community that enhances and promotes the content and features offered by the site.

12.Assigning roles and permissions and managing permissions in Drupal

Drupal, a very popular open-source content management system used by many websites around the world, offers a solid and flexible structure for assigning roles and permissions to users within the system. This functionality is extremely important to ensure the security and effective management of content on a website.

In Drupal, roles are predefined categories of users that have specific permissions within the system. For example, an "administrator" role will have full access and control over every part of the website, while a "writer" role may only have permission to create new content but not publish it directly on the site.

Managing roles and permissions in Drupal is very simple and intuitive. Site administrators can create new roles and assign them specific permissions through the Drupal user interface.

They can also modify the permissions assigned to default or custom roles at any time to adapt them to the specific needs of the website.

Once roles are created and permissions are assigned, administrators can then assign the various roles to registered users of the website. This is done through the user management page in Drupal, where they can select the desired roles for each user and save them.

Managing permissions in Drupal goes beyond assigning roles and permissions. Site administrators can also create custom permission rules to control access to specific parts of the site or limit the actions users can take on certain content.

This advanced level of permission management in Drupal is made possible through the Access Control List (ACL) module, which allows administrators to create complex and detailed authorization rules to meet the specific needs of the website.

For example, an administrator may want to grant access to edit certain content only to users with a specific role or to people belonging to a specific group. This level of fine control allows administrators to fully customize the user experience and protect sensitive data within the system.

Additionally, Drupal also offers the ability to control permissions on page elements, such as blocks, form fields, and content types. This allows administrators to restrict access to certain page elements based on the website's needs and ensure greater security and control over content management.

Assigning roles and permissions and managing permissions in Drupal is a fundamental process to ensure the security and effective management of content on a website. The flexibility and power of Drupal's permission management system allow administrators to fully customize the user experience and protect sensitive data within the system.

13. Site Speed Optimization Caching Resource Usage Minimization in Drupal

Improving the loading speed of a website is essential to ensure a good user experience and to improve search engine rankings. Among the most important parameters to optimize a website's speed are caching and minimizing resource usage. In this article, we will delve into how to implement these two practices in a site built with Drupal.

Drupal is a very powerful and flexible content management platform (CMS) used by many large websites. However, its complexity can lead to higher resource demands and slower loading speeds. But with some precautions, it is possible to improve a site's performance on Drupal platforms.

The first practice to adopt to increase the speed of a Drupal site is caching. Caching is a technique that involves temporarily storing data so that it can be quickly retrieved when needed. In Drupal, there are several types of caching that can be activated to improve site performance:

1. Page caching: This feature stores a static version of pages created by Drupal so that they can be served quickly without having to reload every single element. To enable this feature, simply go to the "Settings -> Performance" menu and check the box for page caching.

2. Block caching: Blocks are sections of content that can be inserted into specific positions on pages. Enabling block caching allows them to be stored so they can be reused without reloading each time. This feature is also activated from the "Settings -> Performance" menu.

3. View caching: Views are customized displays of content, shown for example in list or grid form. Cache can also be activated for views to improve site performance.

4. Image caching: Images are one of the elements that have a significant impact on the loading speed of a webpage. Using image caching can reduce loading time by optimizing the weight and resolution of images.

The second practice to adopt to optimize the speed of a Drupal site is minimizing resource usage. This means minimizing the amount of resources required to load a page, such as CSS files, JavaScript, images, and plugins. Here are some tips for minimizing resource usage on a Drupal site:

1. Compress CSS and JavaScript files: Reducing the size of CSS and JavaScript files through compression can significantly improve site performance. There are several Drupal modules that allow automatic compression of these files, such as the CSS and JS Compressor module.

2. Optimize images: As mentioned earlier,

images are one of the elements that have a significant impact on the loading speed of a webpage. Using web-optimized images by reducing weight and dimensions can help improve site performance.

3. Limit the use of plugins and modules: Every additional plugin or module installed on Drupal requires resources to function properly. Limiting the use of non-essential plugins and deactivating unused ones can reduce the server load and improve site speed.

4. Optimize cache management: Regularly checking the active caches on the site and ensuring they are properly configured is essential to ensure proper resource management and improve site performance.

Implementing practices like caching and minimizing resource usage on a site built with Drupal is essential to improve loading speed and ensure a good user experience. By following the above-mentioned tips, it is possible to optimize the performance of a Drupal site and make it faster and more efficient.

14.Drupal Security Tips: Backup and Site Restoration

Here are some tips for backing up and restoring your site in Drupal:

1. Regularly back up your site: It is important to regularly create backup copies of your site to prevent data loss in case of any issues.

2. Use backup modules: Drupal offers several modules and tools to facilitate website backup. Make sure to use a reliable and regularly updated backup module.

3. Store backups in a secure location: Make sure to store your backups in a secure location protected from unauthorized access.

4. Test your backups: It is important to regularly test your backups to ensure they are properly executed and can be successfully

restored if needed.

5. Follow restoration procedures: If an issue occurs with your site, make sure to carefully follow restoration procedures to bring your site back online as soon as possible.

6. Keep your site updated: Make sure to keep your Drupal site updated with the latest versions of modules and the core to ensure the security and stability of your site.

By following these tips and maintaining a regular backup and restoration routine, you can protect your Drupal site from any issues and ensure the continuity of your online activities.

15. SEO Optimization for Drupal

Drupal is a popular content management system (CMS) that offers numerous advanced features for creating and managing websites. However, to get the most benefit from a Drupal site, it is essential to implement a solid search engine optimization (SEO) strategy.

SEO optimization for Drupal involves a series of actions to ensure that the site is easily indexable by search engines and appears in top positions in search results for specific keywords. In this article, we will discuss the key points to consider to optimize a website created with Drupal.

1. Use friendly URLs

One of the first steps to optimize a Drupal site is to use friendly URLs. This means creating URLs that are meaningful to users and contain relevant keywords to the page's content.

Drupal offers the ability to customize page URLs through the Pathauto module, which automatically creates URLs based on the content title.

2. Optimize meta tags

Meta tags are HTML tags that provide information about a web page's content to search engines. Drupal offers the ability to manage meta tags through the Metatag module, which allows you to insert meta tags such as title, description, and keywords for each page on the site. It is important to use relevant keywords in meta tags to improve the site's visibility in search results.

3. Optimize images

Images are an important element of a website's user experience, but it is important to optimize them to ensure they do not slow down page loading. Drupal offers the ability to compress images and add alternative text for images through the ImageAPI Optimize module. Additionally, it is advisable to use keywords in image file names and ALT tags to improve the site's visibility in image search results.

4. Create a responsive site

A responsive site is essential to ensure a good user experience on all devices, both desktop and mobile. Drupal offers many responsive themes that automatically adapt to the user's device screen size. Ensuring the site is mobile-friendly is important to improve site navigation and positioning in mobile search results.

5. Optimize page loading speed

Page loading speed is a key factor for a site's positioning in search results. Drupal offers various options to optimize page loading speed, such as compressing CSS and JavaScript files, page caching, and image optimization. Use tools like Google PageSpeed Insights to test the site's loading speed and implement the suggested recommendations to improve site performance.

6. Optimize page titles

Page titles are one of the most important elements for SEO optimization of a website. Using relevant keywords and accurately describing the page content in the title can help improve the site's positioning in search results. Drupal allows you to customize page titles through the Page Title module, which automatically creates titles based on the page's content.

7. Create an XML site map

An XML site map is a file that lists all the

pages of a website and provides information to search engines on how to navigate the site. Drupal offers the ability to easily create an XML site map through the XML Sitemap module, which allows you to submit the site map to major search engines like Google and Bing to facilitate page indexing.

8. Manage redirects

Redirects are essential to ensure users are redirected correctly to the right pages when page URLs change. Drupal offers the ability to manage redirects through the Redirect module, which allows you to create permanent or temporary redirects for site pages. It is important to eliminate harmful redirects and keep redirects up-to-date to avoid accessibility issues and penalties from search engines.

9. Monitor SEO performance

Once the SEO optimization actions are

implemented, it is important to monitor the site's performance using analytics tools like Google Analytics and Google Search Console. These tools provide detailed information on site traffic, the most used keywords by users, and overall SEO performance. Use this information to identify areas for improvement and implement new strategies to further optimize the site.

SEO optimization for Drupal is essential to improve the visibility and positioning of a website in search results. Implementing a solid SEO optimization strategy can help increase organic traffic to the site, improve user experience, and achieve business goals. By following the suggestions described in this article, significant results can be achieved and the Drupal website can be positioned at the top of search results.

16.Troubleshooting Common Issues for Drupal Access Denied Error, Theme Display Issues, and Database Errors

Drupal is an extremely powerful and flexible open source content management platform, but like all technologies, it can experience technical issues that need to be resolved. In this article, we will explore two common issues that can occur during the development or maintenance of a Drupal site: access denied error and theme display problems.

Access Denied Error:

The access denied error is one of the most common issues users may encounter on Drupal. This error occurs when a user tries to access a page or a resource for which they do not have the necessary permissions. The causes of this error can be multiple, including permissions configuration errors, problems with user roles, or even security breaches.

To resolve this issue, it is important to first check the permissions of the involved users. Make sure the user has the appropriate permissions to access the desired page or resource. You can do this by visiting Drupal's permission management page and checking the permissions associated with the user roles involved. Ensure the user has at least the "View" permission for the resource in question.

If the permissions seem to be configured correctly, it may be helpful to check if there are any additional modules that could be influencing user permissions. Temporarily disable them to see if the issue persists. You may also examine Drupal logs to identify any errors related to denied access and pinpoint the root cause of the problem.

If all the above solutions do not resolve the issue, you may need to seek the assistance of an experienced developer or contact Drupal's technical support for a more advanced resolution of the problem.

Theme Display Issues:

Another common issue users may encounter on Drupal is related to the display of the site's theme. This problem occurs when the website theme is not displayed correctly or when layout or style errors are shown. The causes of this problem can be multiple, including coding errors, conflicts with other modules or themes, or browser cache issues.

To resolve theme display issues, the first step is to examine the theme code to identify any errors or coding problems. Ensure that the theme has been correctly installed and activated on your Drupal site. Also, check for conflicts with other themes or active modules on the site that may affect the theme display.

If the theme appears to be correctly configured, it may be helpful to check for browser cache issues that could impact theme display. Try clearing the browser cache and refreshing the page to see if the problem is resolved.

If theme display issues persist, it may be useful to temporarily disable all modules and check if the problem is resolved. If so, restore the modules one by one to identify the one causing the problem.

If all the above solutions do not resolve the issue, you may need to seek the assistance of an experienced developer or contact Drupal's technical support for a more advanced resolution of the problem.

With proper diagnosis and a solid understanding of common issues, you can successfully address issues like the access denied error and theme display problems on Drupal.

Drupal Glossary:

Theme: a set of template files that determine the visual appearance of a Drupal site.

Module: an add-on component that extends Drupal's functionalities, allowing users to add new features to their site.

Block: an element that can be placed in various points of the page and displays dynamic content, such as a list of recent articles or a contact form.

View: a way to display Drupal content in different formats, such as a list or a grid.

Field: an element that defines the type of data a content can contain, such as a text field, an image, or a date.

Taxonomy: a content categorization system in Drupal that allows users to organize and navigate content more efficiently.

RSS Feed: a web syndication format that allows readers to receive the latest updates from the site.

WYSIWYG: acronym for "what you see is what you get," a text editor that allows users to format text directly on the web page.

Bootstrap: a front-end framework that enables the creation of responsive websites adaptable to different devices.

Cache: a temporary data storage system that improves website performance by reducing the load on the server.

Layout: the arrangement of blocks and content on the page, which can be customized according to the user's needs.

Index